Fantastic Lives

College Bound

Amy K. Hooper

Publishing Credits

Rachelle Cracchiolo, M.S.Ed., *Publisher*
Conni Medina, M.A.Ed., *Managing Editor*
Nika Fabienke, Ed.D., *Series Developer*
June Kikuchi, *Content Director*
Susan Daddis, M.A.Ed., *Editor*
Kevin Pham, *Graphic Designer*

TIME is a registered trademark of TIME Inc. Used under license.

Image Credits: Front cover, Vikram Raghuvanshi/iStock; pp.4–5 AF
Archive/Alamy; p.8 GL Archive/Alamy; pp.8–9, p.10 (top), p.28 (bottom)
Science History Images/Alamy; p.11 (top) Getty Images; p.11 (middle)
Pictorial Press Ltd/Alamy; p.11 (bottom) Kathy deWitt/Alamy; p.14–15
Sueddeutsche Zeitung Photo/Alamy; p.16 (bottom) Peter van Evert/
Alamy; p.17, p.19 Dan Addison/UVA University Communications; p.18
(bottom) Cornelius Poppe/AFP/Getty Images; pp.20–21, p.23 Joe Klamar/
AFP/Getty Images; pp.24–25 WENN Ltd/Alamy; p.26 (bottom) Ian Dagnall
Computing/Alamy; pp.26–27 John Stillwell - WPA Pool/Getty Images;
pp.28–29 ©2010 The Regents of the University of California, through
the Lawrence Berkeley National Laboratory; p.30 Courtesy of NASA;
p.32 (bottom) Lucianna Faraone Coccia/FilmMagic; p.33 Eric Reed; p.36
(bottom) JEP Celebrity Photos/Alamy; pp.36–37, pp.38–39 Chris Walker/
MCT/Newscom; pp.46–47 Checubus/Shutterstock; all other images from
iStock and/or Shutterstock.

Library of Congress Cataloging-in-Publication Data

Names: Hooper, Amy K., author.
Title: Fantastic lives : college bound / Amy K. Hooper.
Description: Huntington Beach, CA : Teacher Created Materials, 2019. |
   Includes index. | Audience: Grade 4 to 6.
Identifiers: LCCN 2017056307 (print) | LCCN 2018011352 (ebook) | ISBN
   9781425854720 (e-book) | ISBN 9781425849962 (pbk.)
Subjects: LCSH: Gifted children--Biography--Juvenile literature. | College
   students--Biography--Juvenile literature. | Education, Higher--Juvenile
   literature.
Classification: LCC LC3993 (ebook) | LCC LC3993 .H63 2018 (print) | DDC
   371.95--dc23
LC record available at https://lccn.loc.gov/2017056307

Teacher Created Materials
5301 Oceanus Drive
Huntington Beach, CA 92649-1030
www.tcmpub.com
ISBN 978-1-4258-4996-2
© 2019 Teacher Created Materials, Inc.

Table of Contents

Brain Power

Have you watched the television show *The Big Bang Theory*? It's about four scientists, and one of them is really smart. Sheldon Cooper is very curious, and he knows a lot about **physics**. You probably have heard about a real physicist named Albert Einstein. Many years ago, he asked all kinds of questions about science. He also suggested answers called **theories**.

Albert Einstein is considered to have been a genius. He loved learning and, as a teenager, attended a university in Switzerland. Today, many students go to college to pursue their love of learning. Some people start when they are very young. Their curiosity is off the charts!

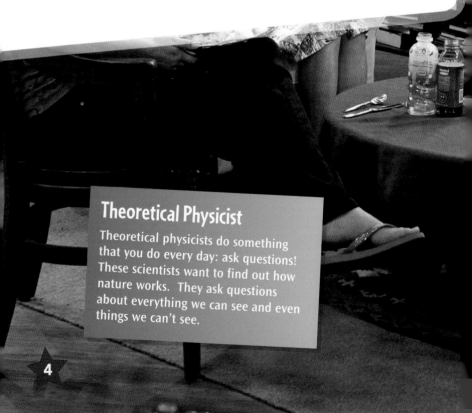

Theoretical Physicist

Theoretical physicists do something that you do every day: ask questions! These scientists want to find out how nature works. They ask questions about everything we can see and even things we can't see.

scene from *The Big Bang Theory*

What does IQ mean?

The intelligence quotient (IQ) is one way that we try to measure how someone thinks and solves problems. After you take a bunch of tests, you receive a score. Most people earn a score between 90 and 100.

Young Geniuses

Who are these young students who graduate early from high school and earn college degrees? You might have more in common with them than you might think.

In this book, you'll meet six brilliant students. On page 16, you can read about Gregory Smith, who earned a diploma from a public high school in Florida when he was 9 years old.

Some of the featured students were homeschooled. Belicia Cespedes liked studying at home because she could learn as quickly as she wanted. Her story is on page 32.

Wherever these students learned, they also played sports, hung out with friends, and played musical instruments. Sho Yano began writing classical music on the piano by the age of 5. His story is on page 36. Yano isn't the only smart one in his family. His sister earned a biology degree at the age of 13.

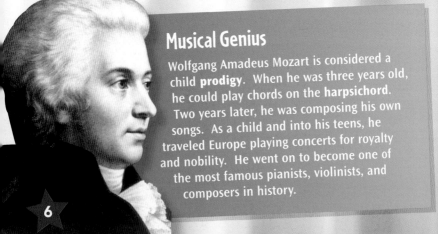

Musical Genius

Wolfgang Amadeus Mozart is considered a child **prodigy**. When he was three years old, he could play chords on the **harpsichord**. Two years later, he was composing his own songs. As a child and into his teens, he traveled Europe playing concerts for royalty and nobility. He went on to become one of the most famous pianists, violinists, and composers in history.

Other scholars have super smart brothers and sisters, too. Anne-Marie Imafidon is a math whiz and is one of five remarkably bright siblings. You can read about her on page 24.

Team sports, such as soccer, appeal to Moshe Kai Cavalin, who also practices martial arts and has won competitions. Cavalin started college when he was only 8. His story is on page 20.

Another homeschooled scholar, Polite Stewart Jr., also practices martial arts. He finished college at 18, the age most students start college! You can read Stewart's story on page 28.

No matter what you try to do, a big factor is hard work. If you really focus on a subject, you can learn so much!

Maybe not "Genius"

It's not just intelligence that drives these young geniuses. They also share a trait: **perseverance**. As Albert Einstein said, "Genius is one percent talent and 99 percent hard work."

In 1952, Hopper works on a computer.

Grace Hopper

This math whiz became a computer programmer while she was in the military. In the 1940s, Hopper began working on computers during World War II. Now, there's an annual event named after her, where women from around the world talk about technology.

Really Smart Thinkers

This list includes some people who have found answers or created art that is important today.

Ibn Al-Haytham: born 965 in Iraq (math and science)

Al-Haytham is famous for his work in how the eye works. His picture is on an Iraqi bill that is used today.

Michelangelo: born 1475 in Italy (painting, sculpture, architecture)

Michelangelo is considered one of the greatest artists of all time. His masterpieces are among some of the most famous works of art in existence.

Galileo: born 1564 in Italy (science)

Galileo created a telescope that let scientists study other planets. He also discovered four of Jupiter's moons.

Sor Juana Ines de la Cruz: born 1651 in Mexico (literature)

Sor Juana taught herself languages, philosophy, math, and history. She lived her life as a nun and is now known as the first feminist to be published.

Clara Schumann: born 1819 in Germany (pianist, composer)

Schumann did not speak until she was four years old, but had mastered the piano by the age of seven. She began composing when she was 10. Schumann was one of the first pianists to play from memory while performing.

Wole Soyinka: born 1934 in Nigeria (literature)

In 1986, Soyinka became the first African to be awarded the Nobel Prize for Literature.

College Life

Imagine if you started taking classes at a college campus away from home right now. What would that be like? How would you feel if you were a lot younger than everyone else?

Advice and Activities

In some cases, a young scholar might go to class with a parent or another adult sitting nearby. For other prodigies, taking one course to start sometimes helps ease the transition to college.

Other adults also might help a younger student. Some professors act as mentors and meet with these young students regularly. Professors often ask about how the students are doing in their classes as well as about their lives outside school.

Different Degrees

There are different kinds of college degrees.

* Associate's degree—usually finished in 2 years
* Bachelor's degree—usually finished in 4 years
* Master's degree—earned after a bachelor's degree; finished in 2–3 years, but time may vary
* Doctoral degree—earned after a master's degree; time to finish varies

THINK LINK

❯ How do you define *genius*?

❯ Why is curiosity important?

Quirky Clubs

Some colleges offer unique clubs. At the Massachusetts Institute of Technology, there is a club for underwater hockey! It's played at the bottom of a pool with a puck and short stick. The University of Michigan is known for its Squirrel Club. Members meet a couple of times a week to feed peanuts to squirrels on campus. The squirrels will take the nuts right from a feeder's hand!

Teams battle during an underwater hockey match.

Young students have opportunities to be a part of college life. Joining clubs is a great way to get involved on campus. Clubs range from academic pursuits, such as mock trial, to social activities, such as ballroom dancing. Some groups are part of a short-term service project or help plan a campus event. Students can also be research assistants for professors in their area of study.

Sadly, some parts of college may not be positive. Strangers might write mean comments about young scholars on social media sites. Others might say cruel things directly to these students. And some people do not want to hear from gifted but younger thinkers in their classes or on campus. Bullying and **intimidation** are not acceptable in any setting.

You Are Under Oath

Mock trial clubs are intended to teach students about the judicial system. Teams from around the country compete against each other. There are usually six members on a team. Three members act as lawyers, and the other three are witnesses.

Brains and Compassion

When he was 10 years old, Gregory Robert Smith started going to a private college in Virginia. His classmates were at least seven years older than he was. He earned a degree in math when he was 13. Then, he finished more difficult degrees in math and biology.

Smith earned his fourth degree when he was 26. He started working in a laboratory so he could study **genes** and create better medicines.

In the Public Eye

Smith's life in the public spotlight began early. As a young boy, he talked with many people about children's rights around the world.

Nobel Peace Prize

Alfred Nobel, a Swedish man, created the Nobel Peace Prize in 1901. The winner of the award is selected by a committee in Norway. The winner is called the Peace Prize **Laureate.**

Computational Biology

In 2009, Smith earned his master's degree in computational biology. This field of study combines computers and biology. It began in the 1950s. Scientists use computers to study test results from experiments. They use the results to help answer questions.

Gregory Smith

Smith spoke about children's safety and health. He went to events like the United Nations Special Session on Children. During his travels and speeches, Smith met world leaders. He met Nelson Mandela from South Africa and Mikhail Gorbachev from the former Soviet Union. Smith wanted people in power to pay more attention to children. That's why he spoke at the "Say Yes for Children" campaign, which began in 2002.

His charity work tied into his learning skills. "I believe I've been given a special gift," Smith said in a 1999 interview. "I don't know how or why I've been given it, but I want to use it to the best of my abilities to help mankind."

Speaking up for Education

In 2014, Malala Yousafzai (mah-LAH-lah yoo-sahf-ZAY) won the Nobel Peace Prize. At 17, she was the youngest person to win the award. She is an activist for children's access to education.

As of 2017, Smith is researching genes to produce better medicines.

Model United Nations

In 1945, world leaders created the United Nations. Their purpose was to work together toward peace. High school students can try their hand at promoting peace in a program called Model United Nations. They learn about the ways that political leaders work on problems that affect everyone.

The Sky Is Not a Limit

Moshe Kai Cavalin was homeschooled until he was 8 years old. That's when he enrolled in college. He was allowed to take only two classes at first because of his age. By the time Cavalin was 15, he had a degree in math. After that, he finished a degree in computer security and started on a business degree. He's so good at math and with computers that he passed a test that allows him to lawfully **hack** into computer systems.

Persistence Is Important

One of Cavalin's dreams was to work for the National **Aeronautics** and Space Administration (NASA). It is the official space program of the United States. Cavalin wanted to be an **intern** at NASA. He wasn't accepted at first because he was too young. But when he was 17, Cavalin was invited to work at a NASA center.

Cavalin enrolled at UCLA (shown here) when he was 8 years old.

Ethical Hacking

Cavalin is a Certified Ethical Hacker (CEH). He passed a difficult test to earn a CEH **credential**. The certification program ensures that the good guys can find problems in computer systems before bad guys do.

Cavalin worked at NASA for a year. He worked on computer programs that keep airplanes and drones from hitting objects.

Successful Author

In 2011, Cavalin wrote his first book, *We Can Do*, to help students see how he learned to study. In the book, he outlines how anyone with **discipline**, focus, and determination can succeed in school.

Soon, Cavalin heard from thousands of students who had read *We Can Do*. Some of these students had been bullied. Cavalin published a second book, *Bully Down*, in 2015. He shared his experiences with bullies and tried to help other kids feel less alone and more confident.

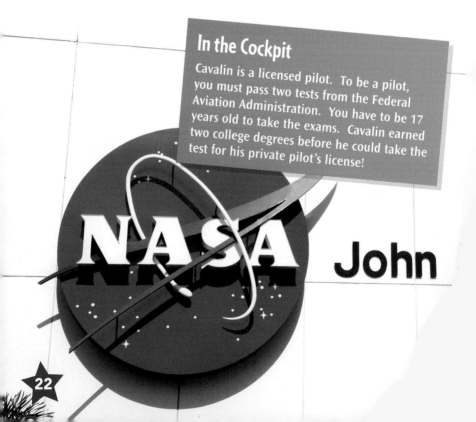

In the Cockpit

Cavalin is a licensed pilot. To be a pilot, you must pass two tests from the Federal Aviation Administration. You have to be 17 years old to take the exams. Cavalin earned two college degrees before he could take the test for his private pilot's license!

NASA John

The Bully Project

In 2011, a documentary called *Bully* debuted. The film opens on the first day of school. It follows five students who are being bullied. It shows how bullying affects victims and their families. It also shines a light on bullies and the people who stand by quietly and do nothing. *Bully* brought much-needed attention to this big problem in schools across the country.

Cavalin holds copies of his book, *We Can Do*, published in different languages.

Adept at Maths

Anne-Marie Imafidon lives in England. In this part of the world, people refer to math as *maths*. And maths is just one of the subjects that Imafidon loves. When she was 10, she passed two tests in maths and technology that most British students take when they're 16.

When she was 11, Imafidon passed harder tests in computing. In 2003, she received an award to study maths in the United States. After returning to Britain, she earned another degree in maths and computer science by the time she was 20.

A Role Model

Imafidon often says she likes maths, technology, and helping others. In fact, she helped create a program called STEMettes. It supports British girls who want to learn about science, technology, **engineering**, and math (STEM). It offers activities and helps girls talk to mentors. The program has earned awards, too.

Her Passion for Tech

"One of the main reasons why I love technology and why I run STEMettes is because I'm a really creative person, and technology allows me to be really creative."— Anne-Marie Imafidon

pictured from left to right: Samantha, Peter, Anne-Marie, and Paula Imafidon

Smart Siblings

Imafidon has three sisters and a brother. They are also incredibly smart. They are known as "Britain's Brainiest Family!"

Imafidom has also received awards. In 2017, the British government gave her the Member of the Order of the British Empire (MBE). She was given the award for all of her work with young women. Now, she can show off that honor by putting those initials after her name—Anne-Marie Imafidon, MBE.

Why STEM?

Fewer women than men work in STEM jobs. That's part of why Imafidon wants to encourage girls as young as 5 to think about technical careers.

Some of the most popular STEMette events are **hackathons**. Girls spend a day or two learning and writing computer codes.

"With STEMettes, we try to suspend reality," Imafidon says. "Normally, you might not see 50 girls all coding or building or investigating. But when you're with us, it's going to be the most normal thing ever."

Ada Lovelace

In 1843, Ada Lovelace translated an academic article from Swiss to English and added her own notes. In this work, she wrote about codes using symbols, letters, and numbers to be used in a device known now as the computer. She died in 1852 with little recognition. But today she is known as the first computer programmer. Ada Lovelace Day is the second Tuesday of October.

Imafidon smiles proudly after receiving her MBE.

Royal Rewards

The MBE is one of three awards created by King George V. He introduced them in 1917 as a way to reward soldiers and civilians for their contributions during World War I. The highest award is the Commander of the Order of the British Empire (CBE). Next is the Officer of the Order of the British Empire (OBE). People can now receive them for a variety of reasons.

Engineering the Future

The first thing to know about Polite Stewart Jr. is that his first name is pronounced "POH-leet." The second thing to know about this Louisiana native is that he really likes science! He earned a degree in physics from Southern University Baton Rouge when he was 18 years old. He later returned to that school to finish degrees in two branches of engineering.

At Home in the Lab

Stewart has spent a lot of time in labs around the country. At 19, he went to work at the Berkeley Lab in Berkeley, California. He was one of the lab's youngest employees ever. Stewart worked with X-rays and on different projects. He enjoyed working in an environment where he felt he belonged. "I've never felt normal before. I've never felt not different," he said. He stayed at the lab for two years before going back to school in Louisiana.

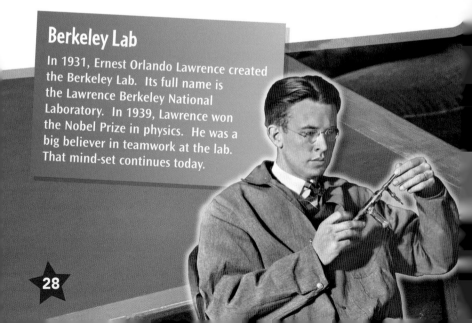

Berkeley Lab

In 1931, Ernest Orlando Lawrence created the Berkeley Lab. Its full name is the Lawrence Berkeley National Laboratory. In 1939, Lawrence won the Nobel Prize in physics. He was a big believer in teamwork at the lab. That mind-set continues today.

Another Physics Fan

When he was a young student, Einstein began asking lots of questions. As a teenager, he became very curious about light and magnetic fields. He won a Nobel Prize for physics in 1921.

During the summer, Stewart returned to the West Coast. This time, he worked in a lab in the state of Washington. He was an engineering intern at Pacific Northwest National Laboratories. Many years ago, NASA asked that lab to test some of the materials collected on the moon by American astronauts. This lab also helped create the process for making compact discs. Its motto is "Discovery in Action." That sounds perfect for a curious person like Stewart.

What's Next?

Stewart says he wants to work as a **biomedical** engineer. In this field, he can combine his engineering education with medicine. Stewart might create **health care** equipment that can help many people stay healthy and enjoy life.

Moon Dust

In 1969, American astronauts walked on the moon for the first time. They came back to Earth with pieces of the moon's surface. These pieces were tested for **radioactive** atoms.

STOP! THINK...

The table below shows salaries for the main fields of engineering and how much those fields are expected to grow by 2024. Use the information in the table to answer the following questions.

> Which type of engineering job is projected to have the most job growth?

> Based on the salary and projected growth, which field of engineering would you choose to go into? Explain your reasoning.

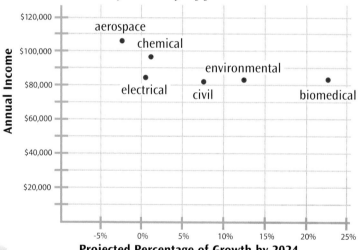

Engineering Opportunities

Financial Whiz

Numbers always made a lot of sense to Belicia Cespedes when she was growing up. She graduated from high school at age 13. Then, she wanted to take some fun classes online. One of them was about bookkeeping. A bookkeeper keeps track of the money that a business spends and earns. And that's when Cespedes discovered her future career.

Cespedes earned a bachelor's degree in **accounting** and began working as an accountant. She later earned a master's degree in accounting.

A Big Certificate

Before Cespedes started working on her second degree, she studied to take four tests. If she passed all four exams, she would get a certified public accounting (CPA) license.

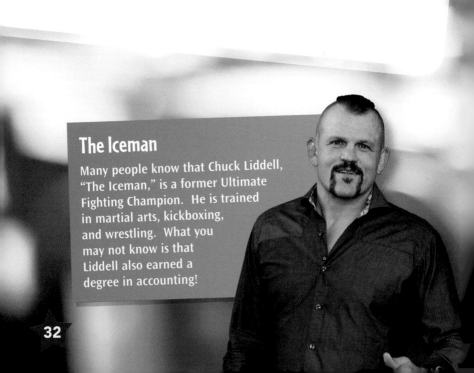

The Iceman

Many people know that Chuck Liddell, "The Iceman," is a former Ultimate Fighting Champion. He is trained in martial arts, kickboxing, and wrestling. What you may not know is that Liddell also earned a degree in accounting!

Belicia Cespedes

CPAs

CPAs help people with taxes and give advice to businesses. They even search for evidence of crimes. To stay up-to-date on current accounting procedures and trends, CPAs must continue taking classes.

The first time that Cespedes took the CPA tests, she did not pass. She studied more, took the tests again, and passed all four parts! At 17 years old, Cespedes became one of the youngest people in the world to earn a CPA license.

A Young Voice

Cespedes wants to show that young accountants are important in her **profession**. She is a member of several business organizations. She likes to encourage more young people who are interested in accounting to feel excited and to do their best. Cespedes often gives speeches at business events and shares photos and information on social media. She also writes articles and answers questions from readers.

One of her first jobs was as a **forensic** accountant at an important accounting firm. It has offices all over the world.

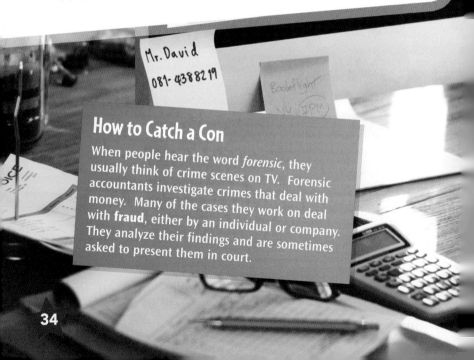

How to Catch a Con

When people hear the word *forensic*, they usually think of crime scenes on TV. Forensic accountants investigate crimes that deal with money. Many of the cases they work on deal with **fraud**, either by an individual or company. They analyze their findings and are sometimes asked to present them in court.

I	J	K	L
Apr-16	May-16	Jun-16	Jul-16
16,392	12,357	20,775	24,766
374	534	-	-
1,850	543	764	133
23	456	246	346
18,639	13,890	25,326	25,599
1,200	1,286	1,500	4,600
900	580	4,252	3,674
-	4,500	6,800	7,550
0,100	5,312	10,252	15,074
134	357	2,466	-
612	453	355	-
,890	13,555	24,890	45,780
234	425	236	3,688
34	346	865	3,467
,904	15,136	28,812	56,965
009	1,367	247	478
120	145	207	109
500	100	500	770
746	462	678	346
375	2,074	1,632	1,703
392	12,357	20,775	24,766
374	534	-	133
350	543	764	346
23	456	246	25,599
39	13,890	25,326	4,600
00	1,266	1,500	3,67
00	580	4,252	

Famous Case

One of the most famous forensic accountants was Frank Wilson. He helped bring down crime boss Al Capone. Wilson and his team went through almost two million documents. They found three records that proved Capone didn't pay taxes on money he earned. Wilson tracked the person who wrote the records by analyzing the handwriting. Capone went to trial and was sentenced.

Kid Doctor

Sho Yano likes to go wherever his interests might take him. Born in Oregon, he lived in California and finished a college degree in Illinois at 13. Then, he started working on a degree in genetics. He also began taking classes to become a doctor.

In the 1990s, there was a TV show called *Doogie Howser, M.D.* It was about a 16-year-old boy doctor. Some people at medical schools thought the show was very unrealistic.

Some people did not like the idea of a teenage student at their medical schools. Most students start medical school when they are 23. Many schools did not want to admit Yano.

From Doctor to Comedy

You might know actor Ken Jeong from his TV show, *Dr. Ken.* Jeong earned his medical degree in 1995. He went to medical school while he developed his stand-up comedy act. Instead of opening a practice, Jeong headed to Los Angeles. He's been in several movies. *Dr. Ken* aired from 2015 to 2017.

The Piano Child

Yano is also an accomplished pianist. His mother noted his gift when he was just 3 years old. She became frustrated playing a waltz by Chopin. She left the room to take a break. She heard the waltz she was trying to play and ran back into the room. There was Yano, playing. By the next year, he was composing music on his own.

Yano checks a patient's reflexes while training to be a doctor.

But a university in Chicago said yes to Yano. He began taking classes there when he was 12 years old. He earned a Ph.D. before earning his M.D. by the age of 21.

But Yano still had more to learn. Brand-new doctors need to finish an internship called a **residency**. Yano chose to study **neurology**. He wants to help children who have problems in their brains and spinal cords.

Smarts for Good

When Yano finished his medical degree, he became the second-youngest person to become a doctor. According to *Guinness World Records*, a 17-year-old has held the record since 1995. But Yano was not aiming to break a record.

Instead, he studied **pediatric** neurology so he can help people. "I'd love to make a great contribution," he said after finishing his degree. "We'll just have to see where life takes me."

What Matters

Being a scholar isn't just about being smart. "I never felt that having a [high] IQ meant you will succeed or not succeed," Yano said. "If I had a good life, if I could have contributed something, that's what really matters."

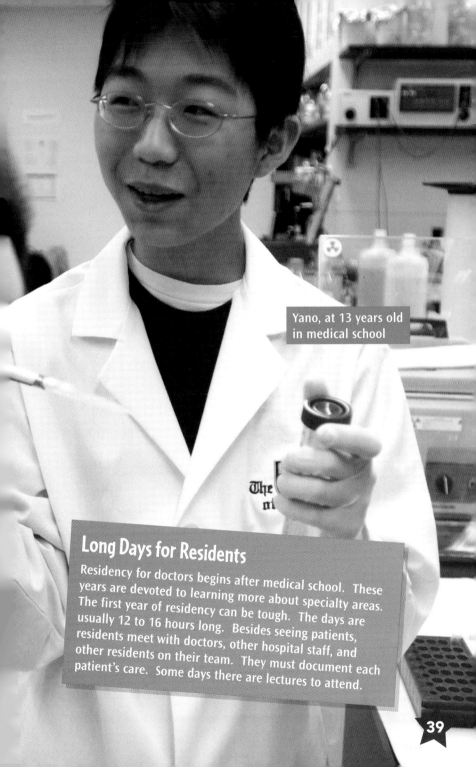

Yano, at 13 years old in medical school

Long Days for Residents

Residency for doctors begins after medical school. These years are devoted to learning more about specialty areas. The first year of residency can be tough. The days are usually 12 to 16 hours long. Besides seeing patients, residents meet with doctors, other hospital staff, and other residents on their team. They must document each patient's care. Some days there are lectures to attend.

Follow Your Curiosity

Very few people are as gifted as the young people profiled in this book. But the important thing to remember is that each of these young scholars pursued their passions. Some were interested in numbers while others enjoyed engineering and science.

That's what we all should do: find the things that we excel at and that we really enjoy doing. If we do this, studying these subjects in high school, college, and beyond will be more gratifying.

If you're not sure what your passion is, then keep searching. Explore different topics until you find the ones that make your brain say, "Yes! Let's definitely dive into this!" Then, see where your curiosity leads you!

Plenty of Plays and Poems

William Shakespeare was a prolific writer. He wrote more than 30 plays and more than 150 poems. He lived in England more than 400 years ago but still entertains millions of people. Have you heard of his plays *Romeo and Juliet* or *Hamlet*?

Ask Your Librarian

Someone who can help you find good information quickly is a librarian. Look for one at your school or a local library. They're waiting for a chance to give you a hand!

Glossary

accounting—the system or job of keeping financial records; similar to bookkeeping

aeronautics—a type of science about airplanes and flying

biomedical—related to biological, medical, and physical science

credential—a document that proves a person is qualified to do a certain job

discipline—the power to keep working on something even when it is difficult

engineering—types of jobs that use scientific methods to design and create big things or new products

forensic—using scientific methods to investigate or solve crimes

fraud—a crime in which a person takes something from another in a dishonest way

genes—parts of a cell that affect the growth of a living thing

hack—to secretly get access to files on a computer or computer network, sometimes not for a good purpose

hackathons—events where computer programmers work together, often to create good software

harpsichord—an instrument resembling a piano that has strings that are plucked

health care—the prevention or treatment of illness by different kinds of doctors

intern—a student or recent graduate who continues learning while working at a job

intimidation—making someone afraid by threats

laureate—someone who won an important prize or honor for achievement

neurology—the study of the nervous system and diseases that affect it

pediatric—related to the medical care of children

perseverance—the trait that allows someone to keep working even in difficult times

physics—a science about the way that heat, light, electricity, and sound act

prodigy—young person who is unusually talented in some way

profession—a type of job that requires certain training and skills

prolific—producing a large amount

radioactive—having a powerful, dangerous form of energy called radiation

residency—a time when a doctor works in a hospital to learn more about a type of medicine

theories—ideas that might be true but are not proven to be true

Index

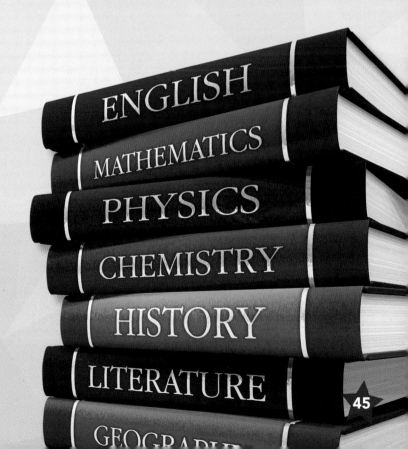

Check It Out!

Books

Fenner, Carol. 1997. *Yolonda's Genius*. New York: Aladdin Paperback.

Gout, Leopoldo. 2016. *Genius: The Game*. New York: Feiwel & Friends.

Lynne, Jenny. 2013. *Kid Docs*. CreateSpace Independent Publishing Platform.

Robledo, I. C. 2016. *The Secret Principles of Genius: The Key to Unlocking Your Hidden Genius Potential*. CreateSpace Independent Publishing Platform.

Videos

DeVito, Danny. 1996. *Matilda*. TriStar Pictures.

Foster, Jodie. 1991. *Little Man Tate*. Orion Pictures.

Ree, Benjamin. 2016. *Magnus*. Moskus Film.

Websites

Mensa. Mensa International. www.mensa.org.

TED. *Ideas Worth Sharing*. www.ted.com.

Try It!

Choose an interest or talent you have. It might be skateboarding, playing an instrument, or a subject at school. Put together a how-to book that teaches others about your amazing ability and how they, too, can develop it.

★ What interest or talent do you have that you want to share with others?

★ Think about the steps you had to take to improve and become an expert.

★ Write and illustrate each step. You may also use diagrams and labels. Remember to use adjectives and adverbs that describe each step.

★ Create a clever title for your work.

★ Share with your classmates!

About the Author

College was one of Amy K. Hooper's favorite times of her life. She learned so much about many subjects, and she made many friends. Amy graduated with a journalism degree from a state university. Then, she kept learning about publishing from really smart coworkers and friends. She likes to travel because it introduces her to new places and ideas.